A **Love**
Treasury

A Love Treasury

EDITED BY David Baird

Andrews McMeel Publishing

Kansas City

FIRST PUBLISHED BY

MQ Publications Limited
12 The Ivories,
6-8 Northampton Street,
London N1 2HY

Copyright © 2002 by MQ PUBLICATIONS LIMITED
Selection and biographical text © 2002 by DAVID BAIRD

DESIGN BY **balley design associates**

ISBN:0-7407-2899-7
Library of Congress Control Number: 2002107699

PRINTED AND BOUND IN CHINA

1 3 5 7 9 0 8 6 4 2

contents

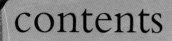

falling in love **7**

discovering each other **49**

love in full bloom **89**

marriage **129**

when love goes wrong **171**

lasting love **211**

falling in l♡ve

Everyone falls in love at some point in their lives, but no matter how often it has happened throughout history, it is still a unique and magical experience for the two people involved. In this section, we see the different ways people fall in love, how they make their first tentative declarations. and the feelings of delirium caused by the first kiss.

Falling in love consists merely in uncorking the imagination and bottling the common-sense.

HELEN ROWLAND

You can't blame gravity for falling in love.

ALBERT EINSTEIN

Longing

Come to me in my dreams, and then
By day I shall be well again.
For then the night will more than pay
The hopeless longing of the day.

Come, as thou cam'st a thousand times,
A messenger from radiant climes,
And smile on thy new world, and be
As kind to others as to me.

Or, as thou never cam'st in sooth,
Come now, and let me dream it truth.
And part my hair, and kiss my brow,
And say My love! why sufferest thou?

Come to me in my dreams, and then
By day I shall be well again.
For then the night will more than pay
The hopeless longing of the day.

MATTHEW ARNOLD

No one is one. No one's alone. No one's world is **THAT** small.

ROBERT CREELEY

There is no disguise which can hide love for long
where it exists, or simulate it where it does not.

FRANÇOIS, DUC DE LA ROCHEFOUCAULD

1833

I have something stupid and ridiculous to tell you. I am foolishly writing to you instead of having told you this, I do not know why, when returning from that walk.

To-night I shall be annoyed at having done so. You will laugh in my face, will take me for a maker of phrases in all my relations with you hitherto. You will show me the door and you will think I am lying.

I am in love with you. I have been thus since the first day I called on you.

Alfred De Musset

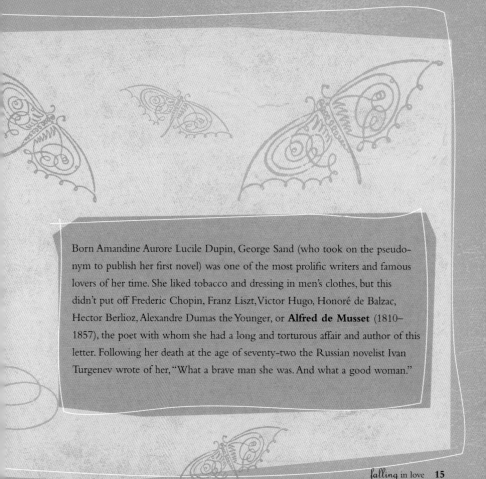

Born Amandine Aurore Lucile Dupin, George Sand (who took on the pseudonym to publish her first novel) was one of the most prolific writers and famous lovers of her time. She liked tobacco and dressing in men's clothes, but this didn't put off Frederic Chopin, Franz Liszt, Victor Hugo, Honoré de Balzac, Hector Berlioz, Alexandre Dumas the Younger, or **Alfred de Musset** (1810–1857), the poet with whom she had a long and torturous affair and author of this letter. Following her death at the age of seventy-two the Russian novelist Ivan Turgenev wrote of her, "What a brave man she was. And what a good woman."

If you would be loved, love and be lovable.

BENJAMIN FRANKLIN

They do not love that do not show their love.

WILLIAM SHAKESPEARE

Little Letter

Go, little letter, apace, apace,
Fly:
Fly to the light of the valley
below—
Tell my wish to her dewy
blue eye.

ALFRED, LORD TENNYSON

The Young Man's Song

I WHISPERED, "I am too young,"
And then, "I am old enough";
Wherefore I threw a penny
To find out if I might love.
"Go and love, go and love, young man,
If the lady be young and fair."
Ah, penny, brown penny, brown penny,
I am looped in the loops of her hair.

O love is the crooked thing,
There is nobody wise enough
To find out all that is in it,
For he would be thinking of love.

Till the stars had run away
And the shadows eaten the moon.
Ah, penny, brown penny, brown penny,
One cannot begin it too soon.

W. B. YEATS

falling in love **21**

Of all forms of caution, caution in love is perhaps the most fatal to true happiness.

BERTRAND RUSSELL

A very small degree of hope is sufficient to cause the birth of love.

STENDHAL

A profound sympathy took immediate possession of my soul. I cannot better explain it to you what I felt than by saying that your unknown heart seemed to pass into my bosom—there to dwell forever—while mine, I thought, was translated into your own. From that hour I loved you. Yes, I now feel that it was then—on that evening of sweet dreams—that the very first dawn of human love burst upon the icy Night of my spirit. Since that period I have never seen nor heard your name without a shiver half of delight, half of anxiety . . . for years your name never passed my lips, while my soul drank in, with a delerious thirst, all that was uttered in my presence respecting you. The merest whisper that concerned you awoke in me a shuddering sixth sense, vaguely compounded of fear, ecstatic happiness, and a wild, inexplicable sentiment that resembled nothing so nearly as the consciousness of guilt.

Edgar Allan Poe (1809–1849), American writer, to Sarah Helen Whitman, American poet, October 1, 1848. His wife had died the previous year, and the distraught Poe wrote feverish letters to both Whitman and a married woman, Anne Richmond. At the time the letter was written, Poe was battling alcoholism and depression, and he was to die a year later.

And when the future hinges on the
next words that are said, don't let
logic interfere, believe your heart
instead.

PHILIP ROBISON

Many a man has fallen in love with a girl in light so dim he would not have chosen a suit by it.

MAURICE CHEVALIER

Thursday morning, 1834

My heart overflows with emotion and joy! I do not know what heavenly languor, what infinite pleasure permeates it and burns me up. It is as if I had never loved!!! Tell me whence these uncanny disturbances spring, these inexpressible foretastes of delight, these divine tremors of love. Oh! all this can only spring from you, sister, angel, woman, Marie! All this can only be, is surely nothing less than a gentle ray streaming from your fiery soul, or else some secret poignant teardrop which you have long since left in my breast.

My God, my God, never force us apart, take pity on us! But what am I saying? Forgive my weakness, how couldst Thou divide us! Thou wouldst have nothing but pity for us. . . . No no! . . . It is not in vain that our flesh and our souls quicken and become immortal through Thy

Word, which cries out deep within us Father, Father . . . it is not in vain that thou callest us, that Thou reachest out Thine hand to us, that our broken hearts seek their refuge in Thee. . . . O! we thank, bless and praise Thee, O God, for all that Thou has given us, and all that Thou hast prepared for us. . . .

This is to be—to be!

In 1833 **Franz Liszt** (1811–1886), Hungarian composer, met the French countess Marie d'Agoult. She was a close friend of George Sand and was a writer herself, under the pseudonym Daniel Stern. They formed a liaison that endured until 1844 and had three children, one of whom, Cosima, became the wife of the German pianist and conductor Hans von Bulow and, later, of the German composer Richard Wagner.

We conceal it from ourselves in vain—
we must always love something. In those
matters seemingly removed from love, the
feeling is secretly to be found, and man
cannot possibly live for a moment without it.

BLAISE PASCAL

You ask me what I thought about
Before we were lovers.
The answer is easy.
Before I met you
I didn't have anything to think about.

FROM *THE LOVE POEMS OF MARICHIKO* > KENNETH REXROTH

Under the Harvest Moon

Under the harvest moon,
When the soft silver
Drips shimmering
Over garden nights,
Death, the gray mocker,
Comes and whispers to you
As a beautiful friend
Who remembers.

Under the summer roses
When the flagrant crimson
Lurks in the dusk
Of the wild red leaves,
Love, with little hands,
Comes and touches you
With a thousand memories,
And asks you
Beautiful, unanswerable questions.

CARL SANDBURG

What
has happened
makes

the world.
Live
on the edge,

looking.

ROBERT CREELEY

1838

Clara,

How happy your last letters have made me—those since Christmas Eve! I should like to call you by all the endearing epithets, and yet I can find no lovelier word than the simple word "dear," but there is a particular way of saying it. My dear one, then, I have wept for joy to think that you are mine, and often wonder if I deserve you.

One would think that no one man's heart and brain could stand all the things that are crowded into one day. Where do these thousands of thoughts, wishes, sorrows, joys and hopes come from? Day in, day out, the procession goes on. But how light-hearted I was yesterday and the day before! There shone out of your letters so noble a spirit, such faith, such a wealth of love!

What would I not do for love of you, my own Clara! The knights of old were better off; they could go through fire or slay dragons to win their ladies, but we of today have to content ourselves with more prosaic methods, such as smoking fewer cigars, and the like. After all, though, we can love, knights or no knights; and so, as ever, only the times change, not men's hearts . . .

Seventeenth-century German composer and pianist **Robert Schumann** (1810–1856) fell deeply in love with his piano teacher's daughter Clara Wieck, and despite Herr Friedrich Wieck's protests, a court ruling granted the consent they sought and the couple were finally married.

One can live magnificently in this world, if one knows how to work and how to love, to work for the person one loves and to love one's work.

LEO TOLSTOY

There is the kiss of welcome and of parting, the long, lingering, loving, present one; the stolen, or the mutual one; the kiss of love, of joy, and of sorrow; the seal of promise and receipt of fulfillment.

THOMAS C. HALIBURTON

The Night-Piece: To Julia

Her eyes the glow-worm lend thee,
The shooting stars attend thee;
And the elves also,
Whose little eyes glow
Like the sparks of fire, befriend thee.

No Will-o'-th'-Wisp mis-light thee,
Nor snake or slow-worm bite thee;
But on, on thy way,
Not making a stay,
Since ghost there's none to affright thee.

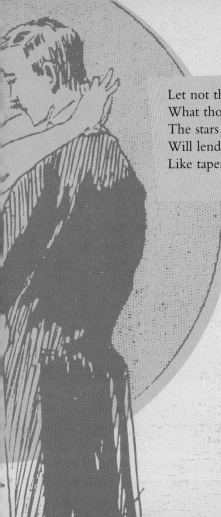

Let not the dark thee cumber;
What though the moon does slumber?
The stars of the night
Will lend thee their light,
Like tapers clear without number.

Then Julia let me woo thee,
Thus, thus to come unto me;
And when I shall meet
Thy silv'ry feet,
My soul I'll pour into thee.

ROBERT HERRICK

I've been so cold and miserable all day, and while working on the good old spuds, the wind has been fearful. All the time I have been thinking of an armchair made for two, in front of a huge crackling fire, the wireless playing some tuneful tunes, and the firelight making shadows on the walls. Fire watching night! A hectic ruff and tumble and then sweet reconciliation. A terribly beautiful hug and then clasped in your arms, my head on your breast, something I am longing for now, a kiss that makes time stand still.

Pamela Moore served in the Women's Land Army during the Second World War. This extract comes from a letter she wrote to her future husband in 1943.

The decision to kiss for the first time is the most crucial in any love story. It changes the relationship of two people much more strongly than even the final surrender; because this kiss already has within it that surrender.

EMIL LUDWIG

Where there is love there is life.

MAHATMA GANDHI

discovering each other

So you've fallen in love—what happens next? This section explores the delicious process of "learning a new heart," the heady period at the beginning of a relationship when you and your new love are constantly together, you feel euphoric and jittery at the same time, and you are beginning to understand that this might be the start of something great.

When we are in love we seem to
ourselves quite different from
what we were before.

BLAISE PASCAL

One is very crazy when in love.

SIGMUND FREUD

5 December, 1839

Dearest,—I wish I had the gift of making rhymes, for methinks there is poetry in my head and heart since I have been in love with you. You are a Poem. Of what sort, then? Epic? Mercy on me, no! A sonnet? No; for that is too labored and artificial. You are a sort of sweet, simple, gay, pathetic ballad, which Nature is singing, sometimes with tears, sometimes with smiles, and sometimes with intermingled smiles and tears.

It is not always easy to find the right words to express the way you feel about someone, as the shy, newly wed **Nathaniel Hawthorne** (1804–1864) discovered when he attempted to put pen to paper in this letter to his wife Sophia Peabody in 1839.

Love . . . does seem to have the faculty of taking your identity away from you and not always in the way the poets mention.

Mary McCarthy (1912–1989), American novelist and critic, from a letter to her friend Hannah Arendt, German-born American philosopher and political theorist, 1961.

Love has features which pierce all hearts, he wears a bandage which conceals the faults of those beloved. He has wings, he comes quickly and flies away the same.

VOLTAIRE

August 10, 1894

We have promised each other—haven't we?—to be at least great friends. If you will only not change your mind! For there are no promises that are binding; such things cannot be ordered at will. It would be a fine thing, just the same, in which I hardly dare believe, to pass our lives near each other, hypnotized by our dreams: your patriotic dream, our humanitarian dream, and our scientific dream.

Of all those dreams the last is, I believe, the only legitimate one. I mean by that that we are powerless to change the social order and, even if we were not, we should not know what to do; in taking action no matter in what direction, we should never be sure of not doing more harm than good, by retarding some inevitable evolution. From the scientific point of view, on the contrary, we may hope to do something; the ground is solider here, and any discovery that we may make, however small, will remain acquired knowledge.

See how it works out: it is agreed that we shall be great friends, but if you leave France in a year it would be an altogether too Platonic friendship, that of two creatures who would never see each other again. Wouldn't it be better for you to stay with me? I know that this question angers you, and that you don't want to speak of it again—and then, too, I feel so thoroughly unworthy of you from every point of view.

Scientist **Pierre Curie** (1859–1906) and his wife Marie shared everything throughout their married lives, including the 1903 Nobel Prize in Physics. Before she finally accepted him as her husband in 1895, however, Marie received many letters of proposal from her enchanted Pierre.

To be in love is to surpass one's self.

OSCAR WILDE

Many people when they fall in love look for
a little haven of refuge from the world,
where they can be sure of being admired
when they are not admirable, and praised
when they are not praiseworthy.

BERTRAND RUSSELL

August 15, 1846

I will cover you with love when next I see you, with caresses, with ecstasy. I want to gorge you with all the joys of the flesh, so that you faint and die. I want you to be amazed by me, and to confess to yourself that you had never even dreamed of such transports. . . . When you are old, I want you to recall those few hours, I want your dry bones to quiver with joy when you think of them.

During a visit to sculptor James Pradier's Paris studio in 1846, French writer **Gustave Flaubert** (1821–1880) first met and fell for the poet Louise Colet. It was hardly a match made in heaven; she was an incredibly jealous woman by nature, a trait which, coupled with Flaubert's stubborn independence, made for a stormy, though passionate, relationship. The couple parted company in 1855.

That one I love who is incapable of ill will,
and returns love for hatred.
Living beyond the reach of I and mine,
and of pain and pleasure,
full of mercy, contented, self-controlled,
with all his heart and all his mind
given to Me—
with such a one I am in love.

FROM *THE BHAGAVAD-GITA*

June 17, 1784

My letters will have shown you how lonely I am. I don't dine at Court, I see few people, and take my walks alone, and at every beautiful spot I wish you were there.

I can't help loving you more than is good for me; I shall feel all the happier when I see you again. I am always conscious of my nearness to you, your presence never leaves me. In you I have a measure for every woman, for everyone; in your love a measure for all that is to be. Not in the sense that the rest of the world seems obscure to me, on the contrary, your love makes it clear; I see quite clearly what men are like and what they plan, wish, do and enjoy; I don't grudge them what they have, and comparing is a secret joy to me, possessing as I do such an imperishable treasure.

You in your household must feel as I often do in my affairs; we often don't notice objects simply because we don't choose to look at them, but things acquire an interest as soon as we see clearly the way they are related to each other. For we always like to join in, and the good man takes pleasure in arranging, putting in order and furthering the right and its peaceful rule. Adieu, you whom I love a thousand times.

In 1784, the German literary genius **Johann Wolfgang von Goethe** (1749–1832) fell in love with Charlotte von Stein, who was seven years his senior, the wife of a Weimar official, and a woman of great charm and talent. She was to be the inspiration for several of Goethe's stage heroines.

I desire love like one desires sleep.

Love makes time pass.
Time makes love pass.

FRENCH PROVERB

August 1873

This last week has seemed an eternity to me; Oh, I wld give my soul for another of those days we had together not long ago. . . . Oh if I cld only get one line from you to reassure me, but I dare not ask you to do anything that your mother wld disapprove of or has perhaps forbidden you to do. . . . Sometimes I doubt so I cannot help it whether you really like me as you said at Cowes you did. If you do I cannot fear for the future tho' difficulties may lie in our way only to be surmounted by patience.

Goodbye dearest Jeannette. My first and only love. . . . Believe me ever to be Yrs devotedly and lovingly,

Randolf S. Churchill

British statesman Randolph Henry Spencer Churchill, best known as Lord Randolph Churchill (1849–1895) married the American heiress Jennie Jerome in 1874. Their son, Winston, was destined to become British prime minister during and beyond World War II. This extract comes from a letter written during their engagement.

A Book of Verse

A book of verse, underneath the bough,
A jug of wine, a loaf of bread—and thou
Beside me singing in the wilderness—
Ah, wilderness were paradise now!

OMAR KHAYYAM

I have enlarged my life by thoughts of you.
Hardly a quarter hour of my waking time
passes without my thinking about you, and
there are many quarter hours in which I do
nothing else.

Franz Kafka (1883–1924), Austrian writer, whose "health is only just good enough for myself alone, not good enough for marriage, let alone fatherhood . . ." writes to his beloved Felice Bauer, circa 1912.

Song: To Celia

Drink to me, only with thine eyes
And I will pledge with mine;
Or leave a kiss but in the cup,
And I'll not look for wine.
The thirst that from the soul doth rise
Doth ask a drink divine:
But might I of Jove's nectar sup
I would not change for thine.

I sent thee late a rosy wreath,
Not so much honouring thee
As giving it a hope that there
It could not withered be
But thou thereon didst only breathe
And sent'st it back to me:
Since, when it grows and smells, I swear,
Not of itself but thee.

BEN JONSON

Love is a punishment. We are punished for
not being able to stay alone.

MARGUERITE YOURCENAR

Love takes off the masks that we
fear we cannot live without, and we
know we cannot live within.

JAMES BALDWIN

One word is too often profaned
For me to profane it,
One feeling too falsely disdained
For thee to disdain it;

One hope is too like despair
For prudence to smother,
And pity from thee more dear
Than that from another.

I can give not what men call love,
But wilt thou accept not
The worship the heart lifts above
And the heavens reject not,—

The desire of the moth for the star,
Of the night for the morrow,
The devotion to something afar
From the sphere of our sorrow?

PERCY BYSSHE SHELLEY

August 1, 1810

Oh My William! it is not in my power to tell thee how I have been affected by this dearest of all letters—it was so unexpected—so new a thing to see the breathing of thy inmost heart upon paper that I was quite overpowered, & now that I sit down to answer thee in the loneliness & depth of that love which unites us & which cannot be felt but by ourselves, I am so agitated & my eyes are so bedimmed that I scarcely know how to proceed . . .

The love letters between English Romantic poet William Wordsworth and his wife **Mary Wordsworth** (1770–1859) reveal a passion that lasted from their earliest days together as schoolchildren until the very end. Mary proved to be his strength and inspiration, a loving mother to their five children, and caring friend to his beloved sister Dorothy, whom she nursed through illness for many years.

If you are ever in doubt as to whether
or not to kiss a pretty girl, always give
her the benefit of the doubt.

THOMAS CARLYLE

A kiss is a lovely trick designed
by nature to stop speech when
words become superfluous.

INGRID BERGMAN

At Last

At last, when all the summer shine
That warmed life's early hours is past,
Your loving fingers seek for mine
And hold them close—at last—at last!
Not oft the robin comes to build
Its nest upon the leafless bough
By autumn robbed, by winter chilled,—
But you, dear heart, you love me now.

Though there are shadows on my brow
And furrows on my cheek, in truth,—
The marks where Time's remorseless plough
Broke up the blooming sward of Youth,—
Though fled is every girlish grace
Might win or hold a lover's vow,
Despite my sad and faded face,
And darkened heart, you love me now!

I count no more my wasted tears;
They left no echo of their fall;
I mourn no more my lonesome years;
This blessed hour atones for all.
I fear not all that Time or Fate
May bring to burden heart or brow,—
Strong in the love that came so late,
Our souls shall keep it always now!

ELIZABETH AKERS ALLEN

love in full bloom

Love, when you are fully immersed in it, is the most wonderful and indescribable feeling. Your body is awakened to the joys of passion, and you take immense pleasure in your lover's company. You feel as though your life has changed and that you are a better person than you were before you loved and were loved. Those feelings of supreme happiness shine out from every extract in this section.

The measure of love is to love without measure.

SAINT AUGUSTINE

Our hours in love have wings; in absence, crutches.

COLLEY CIBBER

My letters! all dead paper, . . . mute and white!—
  And yet they seem alive and quivering
  Against my tremulous hands which loose the string
  And let them drop down on my knee to-night.
  This said, . . . he wished to have me in his sight
  Once, as a friend: this fixed a day in spring
  To come and touch my hand . . . a simple thing,
  Yet I wept for it!—this, . . . the paper's light . . .
  Said, *Dear, I love thee*; and I sank and quailed
  As if God's future thundered on my past.
  This said, *I am thine*—and so its ink has paled
  With lying at my heart that beat too fast.
  And this . . . O Love, thy words have ill availed,
  If, what this said, I dared repeat at last!

FROM *SONNETS FROM THE PORTUGUESE* > ELIZABETH BARRETT BROWNING

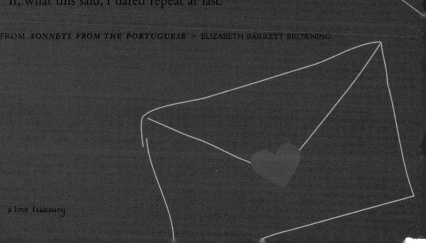

October 2, 1911

I have a thousand images of you in an hour; all different and all coming back to the same. . . . And we love. And we've got the most amazing secrets and understandings. Noel, whom I love, who is so beautiful and wonderful. I think of you eating omelette on the ground. I think of you once against a skyline: and on the hill that Sunday morning.

And that night was wonderfullest of all. The light and the shadow and quietness and the rain and the wood. And you. You are so beautiful and wonderful that I daren't write to you. . . . And kinder than God.

Your arms and lips and hair and shoulders and voice—you.

Rupert Brooke

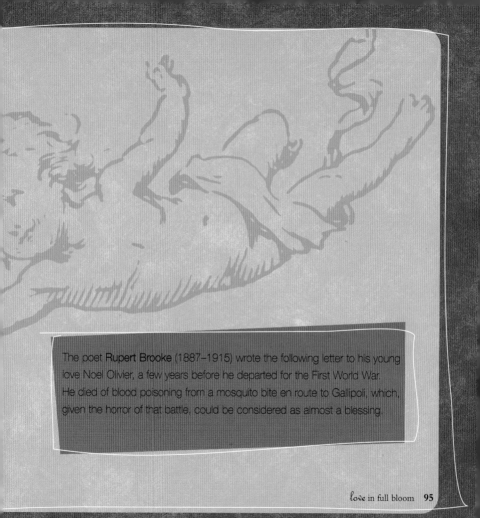

The poet **Rupert Brooke** (1887–1915) wrote the following letter to his young love Noel Olivier, a few years before he departed for the First World War. He died of blood poisoning from a mosquito bite en route to Gallipoli, which, given the horror of that battle, could be considered as almost a blessing.

He who would not be idle, let him fall in love.

OVID

Any thought that is not filled with love seems unholy.

ANDRÉ GIDE

January 27, 1918

My love for you tonight is so deep and tender that it seems to be outside myself as well. I am fast shut up like a little lake in the embrace of some big mountains. If you were to climb up the mountains, you would see me down below, deep and shining— and quite fathomless, my dear. You might drop your heart into me and you'd never hear it touch bottom.

I love you—I love you—Goodnight. Oh Bogey, what it is to love like this!

New Zealand–born writer **Katharine Mansfield** (1888–1923) set up house with the writer and journalist John Middleton Murry just weeks after meeting him at the end of 1911. It was not until 1918, however, that she divorced her first husband, with whom she had never lived, and married Murry. At the time that she wrote this letter, her health was worsening and the couple spent a lot of time apart.

Wild nights—wild nights!
Were I with thee
Wild nights should be
Our luxury!

Futile the winds
To a heart in port—
Done with the compass,
Done with the chart!

Rowing in Eden—
Ah, the sea!
Might I moor, tonight,
In thee!

EMILY DICKINSON

The supreme happiness in life is the conviction that we are loved.

VICTOR HUGO

Sympathy constitutes friendship; but in love there is a sort of antipathy, or opposing passion. Each strives to be the other, and both together make up one whole.

SAMUEL TAYLOR COLERIDGE

The Vine

I dreamed this mortal part of mine
Was metamorphosed to a vine,
Which crawling one and every way
Enthralled my dainty Lucia.
Methought her long small legs and thighs
I with my tendrils did surprise;
Her belly, buttocks, and her waist
By my soft nervelets were embraced.
About her head I writhing hung,
And with rich clusters (hid among
The leaves) her temples I behung,
So that my Lucia seemed to me
Young Bacchus ravished by his tree.
My curls about her neck did crawl,
And arms and hands they did enthrall,
So that she could not freely stir
(all parts there made one prisoner).
But when I crept with leaves to hide
Those parts which maids keep unespied,
Such fleeting pleasures there I took
That with the fancy I awoke;
And found (ah me!) this flesh is mine
More like a stock than like a vine.

ROBERT HERRICK

Bologna, 25 August, 1819

My dearest Teresa,

I have read this book in your garden;—my love, you were absent, or else I could not have read it. It is a favourite book of yours, and the writer was a friend of mine. You will not understand these English words, and others will not understand them,—which is the reason I have not scrawled them in Italian. But you will recognize the handwriting of him who passionately loved you, and you will divine that, over a book which was yours, he could only think of love.

In that word, beautiful in all languages, but most so in yours—Amor mio—is comprised my existence here and hereafter. I feel I exist here, and I feel I shall exist hereafter,—to what purpose you will decide; my destiny rests with you, and you are a woman, eighteen years of age, and two out of a convent. I love you, and you love me,—at least, you say so, and act as if you did so, which last is a great consolation in all events.

But I more than love you, and cannot cease to love you. Think of me, sometimes, when the Alps and ocean divide us,—but they never will, unless you wish it.

George Gordon, Lord Byron (1788–1824) was everything one would expect a world-famous classical poet to be. He was handsome, brilliant if rather reckless, extravagant, and certainly a little debauched. In the words of Matthew Arnold, he was a "romantic hero at odds with the world and calling on all sympathetic readers to view the pageant of his bleeding heart." After divorcing his first wife in 1816 he enjoyed his promiscuous lifestyle, taking love wherever he found it until, at the age of thirty-one, he rediscovered his muse in the form of Teresa, Countess Guiccioli. She was an eighteen-year-old girl married to a wealthy Italian nobleman many years her senior. Byron was, once again, passionately in love.

When Man Enters Woman

When man
enters woman,
like the surf biting the shore,
again and again,
and the woman opens her mouth in pleasure
and her teeth gleam
like the alphabet,
Logos appears milking a star,
and the man
inside of woman
ties a knot
so that they will
never again be separate
and the woman
climbs into a flower
and swallows its stem
and Logos appears
and unleashed their rivers.

This man,
this woman
with their double hunger,
have tried to reach through
the curtain of God
and briefly they have,
though God
in His perversity
unties the knot.

ANNE SEXTON

There is always some madness in love.
But there is also always some reason
in madness.

FRIEDRICH NIETZSCHE

To love someone deeply gives you strength.
Being loved by someone deeply gives you courage.

LAO-TZU

My dearest,

When two souls, which have sought each other for, however long in the throng, have finally found each other . . . a union, fiery and pure as they themselves are . . . begins on earth and continues forever in heaven.

This union is love, true love, . . . a religion, which deifies the loved one, whose life comes from devotion and passion, and for which the greatest sacrifices are the sweetest delights.

This is the love which you inspire in me. . . . Your soul is made to love with the purity and passion of angels; but perhaps it can only love another angel, in which case I must tremble with apprehension.

Yours forever,

Victor Hugo (1821)

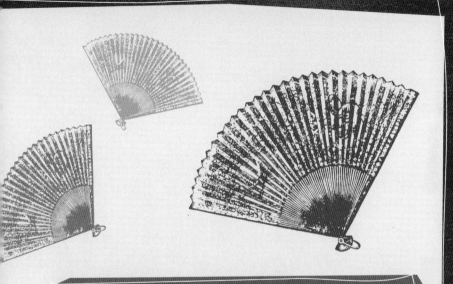

French writer **Victor Hugo** (1802–1885) first met Adele Foucher when he was a teenager, but both their families were opposed to the union, a state of affairs that forced them to become secretly engaged. They had every intention of marrying, and eventually did in 1822, but in the meantime they would carry on their relationship through the exchange of secret messages such as this one.

Naked

Naked, you are simple as a hand,
smooth, earthy, small . . . transparent, round.
You have moon lines and apple paths;
Naked, you are slender as the wheat.

Naked, Cuban blue midnight is your color,
Naked, I trace the stars and vines in your hair;
Naked, you are spacious and yellow
As a summer's wholeness in a golden church.

Naked, you are tiny as your fingernail;
Subtle and curved in the rose-colored dawn
And you withdraw to the underground world

As if down a long tunnel of clothing and of chores:
your clear light dims, gets dressed, drops its leaves,
And becomes a naked hand again.

PABLO NERUDA

A drinking song

Wine comes in at the mouth
And love comes in at the eye;
That's all we know for truth
Before we grow old and die.
I lift the glass to my mouth,
I look at you, and I sigh.

W. B. YEATS

Love is the only passion that
does not suffer a past or future.

HONORÉ DE BALZAC

Whatever our souls are made of, his and mine
are the same.

EMILY BRONTË

February 27, 1913

To "Stella" Beatrice Campbell

I want my rapscallionly fellow vagabond.
I want my dark lady. I want my angel—
I want my tempter.
I want my Freia with her apples.
I want the lighter of my seven lamps of beauty, honour,
laughter, music, love, life and immortality. . . . I want
my inspiration, my folly, my happiness,
my divinity, my madness, my selfishness,
my final sanity and sanctification,
my transfiguration, my purification,
my light across the sea,

my palm across the desert,

my garden of lovely flowers,

my million nameless joys,

my day's wage,

my night's dream,

my darling and

my star . . .

Mrs. Patrick Campbell was the married and stage name of the English actress Beatrice Stella Tanner, for whom Irish-born playwright **George Bernard Shaw** (1856–1950) wrote the leading role in *Pygmalion* (1912). There was much speculation about the nature of their relationship, especially following the publication of their letters in 1952 after their deaths. This passionate plea was written from Shaw to "Stella" in 1913.

London, March 8th, 1760

And now my dear dear Girl let me assure you of the truest friendship for you, that ever Man bore towards a Woman—where ever I am, my heart is warm towards you & ever shall be, till it is cold for ever. I thank you for the kind of proof you gave me of your Love and of yr desire to make my heart easy, in ordering yrself to be denied to You know who—whilst I am so miserable to be separated from my dear dear Kitty, it would have stabb'd my Soul, to have though such a fellow could have the Liberty of coming near you—I therefore take this proof of yr Love & good principles, most kindly—& have as much faith & dependence upon You in it, as if I was at yr Elbow—would to God, I was at it this moment—for I am sitting solitary & alone in my bed Chamber (ten o'clock at night, after the play)—& would give a Guinea for a squeeze of yr hand.

Laurence Sterne (1713–1768), author of *Tristram Shandy*, which is considered to have been the first modern novel, had liaisons with many women in his lifetime. Here he writes to a French singer called Catherine Fourmantel, with whom he began a flirtation while working on the novel.

Love is life. All, everything that I understand, I understand
only because I love. Everything is, everything exists, only
because I love. Everything is united by it alone. Love is God,
and to die means that I, a particle of love, shall return to
the general and eternal source.

LEO TOLSTOY

No love can take the place of love.

MARGUERITE DURAS

He who is in love is wise and is becoming wiser, sees newly every time he looks at the object beloved, drawing from it with his eyes and his mind those virtues which it possesses.

RALPH WALDO EMERSON

marriage

After the euphoria of falling in love and the rituals of the wedding ceremony, comes the settling down into marriage. But marriage is not simply routine and domesticity, and does not represent the end of passion. Instead, as we can see in the extracts in this section, married couples learn to take pleasure in the little things, to appreciate one another's guidance, and delight in the surprise that there is still so much to learn about each other.

A successful marriage requires falling in love many times, always with the same person.

MIGNON MCLAUGHLIN

Love is a driver, bitter and fierce if you fight and resist him,
Easy-going enough once you acknowledge his power.

OVID

First, I send you all the thankes which my heart can conceive, or my words can rehearse for your many travailes, and care taken for me, which though they have not taken effect as you wished, yet my debt to you is not the lesse: but pay it I never shall in this world.

Secondly, I beseech you for the love you bear me living, do not hide your selfe many dayes, but by your travailes seeke to help your miserable fortunes and the right of your poor childe. Thy mourning cannot avail me, I am but dust.

Thirdly, you shall understand, that my land was conveyed bona fide to my childe; the writings were drawne at midsumer was twelve months, my honest cosen Brett can testify so much, and Dolberry too, can remember somewhat therein. And I trust my blood will quench their malice that have cruelly murthered me; and that they will not seek also to kill thee and thine with extreme poverty.

.... my deare wife farewell. Blesse my poore boy. Pray for me, and let my good God hold you both in his arms.

This poignant letter was written by **Sir Walter Raleigh** (1552–1618) to his wife Elizabeth in 1603, believing he would be beheaded the following morning. In the event he gained a reprieve. By a cruel twist of fate, he was actually beheaded fifteen years later, in 1618, on the orders of King James I.

Spring 1919

Sweetheart,

Please, please don't be so depressed—We'll be married soon, and then these lonesome nights will be over forever—and until we are, I am loving, loving every tiny minute of the day and night—Maybe you won't understand this, but sometimes when I miss you most, it's hardest to write—and you always know when I make myself—Just the ache of it all—and I can't tell you. If we were together, you'd feel how strong it is—you're so sweet when you're melancholy. I love your sad tenderness—when I've hurt you—That's one of the reasons I could never be sorry for our quarrels—and they bothered you so—Those dear, dear little fusses, when I always tried so hard to make you kiss and forget—

Scott—there's nothing in all the world I want but you—and your precious love—All the material things are nothing. I'd just hate to live a sordid, colorless existence—because you'd soon love me less—and less—and I'd do anything—anything—to keep your heart for my own—I don't want to live—I want to love first, and live incidentally—Why don't you feel that I'm waiting—I'll come to you, Lover, when you're ready—Don't don't ever think of the things you can't give me—You've trusted me with the dearest heart of all—and it's so damn much more than anybody else in all the world has ever had—

In July 1918, while a soldier stationed in Montgomery, Alabama, F. Scott Fitzgerald met **Zelda Sayre** (1900–1948), the daughter of a Supreme Court judge. The couple fell deeply in love, and as soon as he could, Fitzgerald headed to New York, determined to achieve success as a writer and to marry Zelda. This extract is from a letter Zelda wrote to Fitzgerald during their engagement.

Marriage Morning

Light, so low upon earth,
You send a flash to the sun.
Here is the golden close of love,
All my wooing is done.
Oh, the woods and the meadows,
Woods where we hid from the wet,
Stiles where we stay'd to be kind,
Meadows in which we met!

Light, so low in the vale
You flash and lighten afar,
For this is the golden morning of love,
And you are his morning star.
Flash, I am coming, I come,
By meadow and stile and wood,
Oh, lighten into my eyes and heart,
Into my heart and my blood!

Heart, are you great enough
For a love that never tires?
O' heart, are you great enough for love?
I have heard of thorns and briers,
Over the meadow and stiles,
Over the world to the end of it
Flash for a million miles.

ALFRED, LORD TENNYSON

Paris, December 1795

I wake filled with thoughts of you. Your portrait and the intoxicating evening which we spent yesterday have left my senses in turmoil. Sweet, incomparable Josephine, what a strange effect you have on my heart! Are you angry? Do I see you looking sad? Are you worried? . . . My soul aches with sorrow, and there can be no rest for your lover; but is there still more in store for me when, yielding to the profound feelings which overwhelm me, I draw from your lips, from your heart a love which consumes me with fire? Ah! it was last night that I fully realized how false an image of you your portrait gives!

You are leaving at noon; I shall see you in three hours.

Until then, mio dolce amor, a thousand kisses; but give me none in return, for they set my blood on fire.

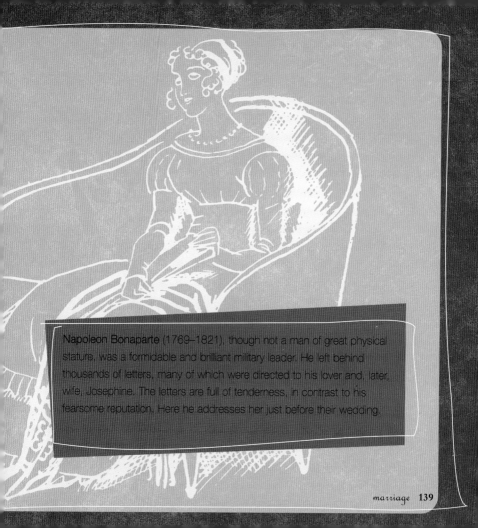

Napoleon Bonaparte (1769–1821), though not a man of great physical stature, was a formidable and brilliant military leader. He left behind thousands of letters, many of which were directed to his lover and, later, wife, Josephine. The letters are full of tenderness, in contrast to his fearsome reputation. Here he addresses her just before their wedding.

Was this the darling I did love?
Was this that mercy from above
did open violets in the spring—
and made my own worn self to sing?

She was. I know. And she is still,
and if I love her? then so I will.
And I will tell her, and tell her right . . .

Oh lovely lady, morning or evening or afternoon.
Oh lovely lady, eating with or without a spoon.
Oh most lovely lady, whether dressed or undressed or partly.
Oh most lovely lady, getting up or going to bed or sitting only.

Oh loveliest of ladies, than whom none is more fair, more gracious, more beautiful.
Oh loveliest of ladies, whether you are just or unjust, merciful, indifferent, or cruel.
Oh most loveliest of ladies, doing whatever, seeing whatever, being whatever.
Oh most loveliest of ladies, in rain, in shine, in any weather.

Oh lady, grant me time,
please, to finish my rhyme.

FROM *BALLAD OF THE DESPAIRING HUSBAND* > ROBERT CREELEY

Mainz, October 17, 1790

PS.—while I was writing the last page, tear after tear fell on the paper. But I must cheer up—catch!—An astonishing number of kisses are flying about—The deuce!—I see a whole crowd of them! Ha! Ha! . . . I have just caught three—They are delicious!—You can still answer this letter, but you must address your reply to Linz, Poste Restante—That is the safest course. As I do not yet know for certain whether I shall go to Regensburg, I can't tell you anything definite. Just write on the cover that the letter is to be kept until called for.

Adieu—Dearest, most beloved little wife—Take care of your health— and don't think of walking into town. Do write and tell me how you like our new quarters—Adieu. I kiss you millions of times.

Wolfgang Amadeus Mozart (1756–1791) crammed a great deal of work into his short life, although it was plagued by poverty and illness. He married Constanze Weber in 1782. This extract is a P.S. added to a letter he wrote her shortly before he died.

One should always be in love. That is
the reason one should never marry.

OSCAR WILDE

No woman marries for money; they are all clever enough, before marrying a millionaire, to fall in love with him first.

CESARE PAVESE

October 3, 1826

. . . it is so easy a thing for you to lift me to
Seventh Heaven! My soul was darker than
midnight, when your pen said "let there be
light" and there was light as at the bidding
of the Word. . . . When I read in your looks
and words that you love me, I feel it in the
deepest part of my soul; and then I care not
one straw for the whole Universe beside . . .

In 1826 Thomas Carlyle married the English woman of letters **Jane Baillie Welsh** (1801–1866), whom he had met in 1821. After 1828, the Carlyles lived on a farm in the quaintly named Craigenputtock, Scotland, where Carlyle was to write his philosophical satire, *Sartor Resartus (The Tailor Retailored)*. This extract is from her last letter to him before they married.

Counting the Beats

You, love, and I,
(He whispers) you and I,
And if no more than only you and I
What care you and I?

Counting the beats,
Counting the slow heart beats,
The bleeding to death of time in
  slow heart beats,
Wakeful they lie.

Cloudless day,
Night, and a cloudless day,
Yet the huge storm will burst upon
  their heads one day
From a bitter sky.

Where shall we be,
(She whispers) where shall we be,
When death strikes home, O where then shall
  we be
Who were you and I?

Not there but here,
(He whispers) only here,
As we are, here, together, now and here,
Always you and I.

Counting the beats,
Counting the slow heart beats,
The bleeding to death of time in slow heart beats,
Wakeful they lie.

ROBERT GRAVES

IN Love, if Love be Love, if Love be ours,
Faith and unfaith can ne'er be equal powers:
Unfaith in aught is want of faith in all.

It is the little rift within the lute,
That by and by will make the music mute,
And ever widening, slowly silence all.

The little rift within the lover's lute,
Or little pitted speck in garnered fruit,
That rotting inward, slowly moulders all.

It is not worth the keeping, let it go.
But shall it? Answer, darling, answer no,
And trust me not at all, or all in all.

FROM *IDYLLS OF THE KING: VIVIEN* > ALFRED, LORD TENNYSON

Habitation

Marriage is not
a house or even a tent

it is before that, and colder:

the edge of the forest, the edge
of the desert
                the unpainted stairs
at the back where we squat
outside, eating popcorn

the edge of the receding glacier

where painfully and with wonder
at having survived even
this far

we are learning to make fire

MARGARET ATWOOD

Women are at last becoming persons first and wives second, and that is as it should be.

MAY SARTON

The most beautiful love means nothing when it is plain; it needs engraving and silversmithing.

GUSTAVE FLAUBERT

My burden, most faithful wife, is a harder one than that which the son of Æson bore. You, too, whom I left still young at my departure from the City, I can believe to have grown old under my calamities. Oh, grant it, ye Gods, that I may be enabled to see you, even if such, and to give the joyous kiss on each cheek in its turn; and to embrace your emaciated body in my arms, and to say, "'twas anxiety, on my account, that caused this thinness"; and, weeping, to recount in person my sorrows to you in tears, and thus enjoy a conversation that I had never hoped for; and to offer the due frankincense, with grateful hand, to the Caesars, and to the wife that is worthy of a Caesar, Deities in real truth!

When Publius Ovidius Naso—known as Ovid (43 B.C.–A.D. 17)—was exiled to Tomis on the Black Sea for displeasing the emperor Augustus, he was separated from his third wife (whose name is unknown) until his death nine years later. Here Ovid compares his sea-journey into exile with the voyage made by Jason and the Argonauts, who risked all in their quest to find the legendary Golden Fleece. In this letter to his wife, he laments the fact that his own troubles are far worse than those Jason experienced.

How to Get a Baby

Go to the sea
the morning after a rainstorm,
preferably
fresh from your man's arms—
the waiwaiwa are drawn
to love-smell.
They are tiny luminous fish
and blind. You must call
the soul of your child
in the name of your ancestors;
Come to me, little fish, come
to Tamala, Tudava, come to me.
Sit in shallow water
up to your waist until the tide
pulls away from you like an exhausted lover.
You will by then
be carrying new life.
Make love that night,
and every night,
to let the little one
who chooses you know
she is one with your joy.

JUDITH ORTIZ COFER

Maybe

Maybe he believes me, maybe not.
Maybe I can marry him, maybe not.

Maybe the wind on the prairie,
The wind on the sea, maybe,
Somebody, somewhere, maybe can tell.

I will lay my head on his shoulder
And when he asks me I will say yes,
Maybe.

CARL SANDBURG

January 1, 1847

My Dearest Husband

. . . I was at that date of marriage a very different being from what I am now and stood in relation to my Heavenly Father in a very different attitude. My whole desire was to live in love, absorbing passionate devotion to one person. Our separation was my first trial—but then came a note of comfort in the hope of being a mother. No creature ever so longed to see the face of a little one or had such a heart full of love to bestow. Here came in trial again sickness, pain, perplexity, constant discouragement—wearing wasting days and nights—a cross, deceitful, unprincipled nurse-husband gone. . . . When you came back you came only to increasing perplexities.

Ah, how little comfort I had in being a mother—how was all that I proposed met and crossed and my may ever hedged up!

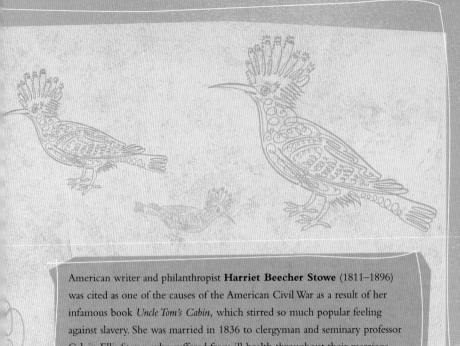

American writer and philanthropist **Harriet Beecher Stowe** (1811–1896) was cited as one of the causes of the American Civil War as a result of her infamous book *Uncle Tom's Cabin*, which stirred so much popular feeling against slavery. She was married in 1836 to clergyman and seminary professor Calvin Ellis Stowe, who suffered from ill health throughout their marriage. Here she reflects upon their life together . . .

There's nothing in the world like the devotion of a married woman. It's a thing no married man knows anything about.

OSCAR WILDE

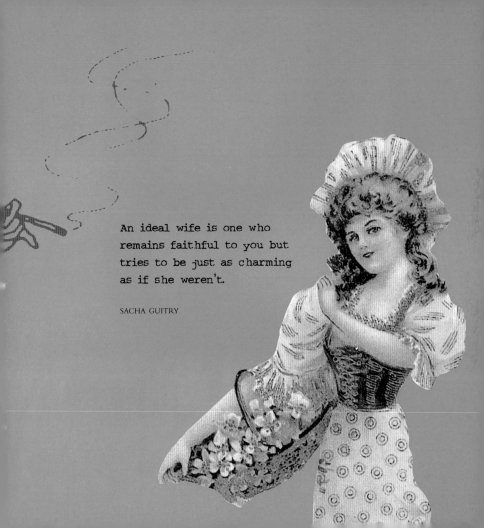

An ideal wife is one who
remains faithful to you but
tries to be just as charming
as if she weren't.

SACHA GUITRY

Flesh of Flesh
Bone of my Bone thou art,
and from thy state
Mine never shall be parted,
weal or woe.

FROM *PARADISE LOST* > JOHN MILTON

XXI.

My perfect wife, my Leonor,
  Oh heart, my own, oh eyes, mine too,
Whom else could I dare look backward for,
  With whom beside should I dare pursue
The path grey heads abhor?

XXII.

For it leads to a crag's sheer edge with
them;
  Youth, flowery all the way, there stops—
Not they; age threatens and they contemn,
  Till they reach the gulf wherein youth
drops,
One inch from life's safe hem!

XXIII.

With me, youth led . . . I will speak now,
  No longer watch you as you sit
Reading by fire-light, that great brow
  And the spirit-small hand propping it,
Mutely, my heart knows how—

XXIV.

When, if I think but deep enough,
  You are wont to answer, prompt as rhyme;
And you, too, find without rebuff
  Response your soul seeks many a time
Piercing its fine flesh-stuff.

FROM *BY THE FIRESIDE* > ROBERT BROWNING

when love goes wrong

People who fall in love don't always live happily ever after. As this section shows, there are many ways in which a relationship can founder—perhaps through infidelity, enforced separation, or just simply "growing apart." Human beings, however, are resilient creatures, and after a break-up most people move on, healed and freshly inspired to love again.

To love and win is the best thing.
To love and lose, the next best.

WILLIAM MAKEPEACE THACKERAY

What then in love can woman do? If we grow fond they
shun us. And when we fly them, they pursue: But
leave us when they've won us.

JOHN GAY

C, 1780

Sophie,

To be with the people one loves, says La Bruyere is enough—to dream you are speaking to them, not speaking to them, thinking of them, thinking of the most indifferent things, but by their side, nothing else matters. O mon amie, how true that is! and it is also true that when one acquires such a habit, it becomes a necessary part of one's existence.

Alas! I well know, I should know too well, since the three months that I sigh, far away from thee, that I possess thee no more, that my happiness has departed. However, when every morning I wake up, I look for you, it seems to me that half of myself is missing, and that is too true.

Twenty times during the day, I ask myself where you are; judge how strong the illusion is, and how cruel it is to see it vanish. When I go to bed, I do not fail to make room for you; I push myself quite close to the wall and leave a great empty space in my small bed. This movement is mechanical, these thoughts are involuntary. Ah! how one accustoms oneself to happiness.

Alas! one only knows it well when one has lost it, and I'm sure we have only learnt to appreciate how necessary we are to each other, since the thunderbolt has parted us. The source of our tears has not dried up, dear Sophie; we cannot become healed; we have enough in our hearts to love always, and, because of that, enough to weep always.

Gabriel

While imprisoned in 1774, the **Comte de Mirabeau** (1749–1791), French politician, met his "Sophie," the Marquise de Monnier, the young wife of an old man. He escaped to Switzerland, where Sophie joined him. When he was caught, he avoided the death sentence for seduction and abduction by submitting to further imprisonment, during which time he wrote this letter.

Love Arm'd

Love in Fantastique Triumph sat,
Whilst bleeding Hearts around him flow'd,
For whom Fresh pains he did create,
And strange Tryanic power he show'd;
From thy Bright Eyes he took his fire,
Which round about, in sport he hurl'd;
But 'twas from mine he took desire,
Enough to undo the Amorous World.
From me he took his sighs and tears,
From thee his Pride and Crueltie;
From me his Languishments and Feares,
And every Killing Dart from thee;
Thus thou and I, the God have arm'd,
And sett him up a Deity;
But my poor Heart alone is harm'd,
Whilst thine the Victor is, and free.

APHRA BEHN

Friendship often ends in love; but love in friendship, never.

CHARLES CALEB COLTON

Love is not love until love's vulnerable.

THEODORE ROETHKE

I loved you; and I probably still do,
And for awhile the feeling may remain—
But let my love no longer trouble you:
I do not wish to cause you any pain.
I loved you; and the hopelessness I knew
The jealousy, the shyness—though in vain—
Made up a love so tender and so true,
As may God grant you to be loved again.

ALEXANDER PUSHKIN

Wednesday Morng. (Kentish Town, 1820)

My Dearest Girl,

I have been for a walk this morning with a book in my hand, but as usual I have been occupied with nothing but you: I wish I could say in an agreeable manner. I am tormented day and night. They talk of my going to Italy. 'Tis certain I shall never recover if I am to be so long separate from you: yet with all this devotion to you I cannot persuade myself into any confidence of you. . . .

You are to me an object intensely desirable—the air I breathe in a room empty of you is unhealthy. I am not the same to you—no—you can wait—you have a thousand activities—you can be happy without me. Any party, anything to fill up the day has been enough.

How have you pass'd this month? Who have you smil'd with? All this may seem savage in me. You do not feel as I do—you do not know what it is to love—one day you may—your time is not come. . . .

I cannot live without you, and not only you but chaste you; virtuous you. The Sun rises and sets, the day passes, and you follow the bent of your inclination to a certain extent—you have no conception of the quantity of miserable feeling that passes through me in a day——Be serious! Love is not a plaything—and again do not write unless you can do it with a crystal conscience. I would sooner die for want of you than—

Yours for ever

J. Keats

The exposure and overexertions of a walking tour in 1818 with his friend Charles Brown brought on the first symptoms of the tuberculosis that would eventually kill **John Keats** (1795–1821). On his return from the tour he returned to London to spend three months nursing his brother Tom through the final stages of the same disease. Here he met and fell in love with a neighbor, Fanny Brawne. His demands upon Fanny, his failing health, and financial uncertainty placed great strains on the couple's relationship, and they were unable to marry. Keats died in Rome in 1821, at the age of twenty-five.

The most dire disaster in love is
the death of imagination.

GEORGE MEREDITH

When a man steals your wife, there is no better
revenge than to let him keep her.

SACHA GUITRY

Could I see you without passion, or be absent from you without pain, I need not beg your pardon for thus renewing my vows that I love you more than health, or any happiness here or hereafter.

Everything you do is a new charm to me, and though I have languished for seven long tedious years of desire, jealously despairing, yet every minute I see you I still discover something new and more bewitching. Consider how I love you; what would I not renounce or enterprise for you?

I must have you mine, or I am miserable, and nothing but knowing which shall be the happy hour can make the rest of my years that are to come tolerable. Give me a word or two of comfort, or resolve never to look on me more, for I cannot bear a kind look and after it a cruel denial.

This minute my heart aches for you; and, if I cannot have a right in yours, I wish it would ache till I could complain to you no longer.

The English playwright and poet **Thomas Otway** (1652–1685) died aged only thirty-three, a broken man with a string of creditors and an unrequited longing for Mrs Elizabeth Barry, who played the leading parts in almost all his plays. His all-absorbing passion for her, as shown in the desperate and wretched tone of this letter, contributed to the ruin of his career, if not his life.

Alas! how light a cause may move
Dissension between hearts that love!
Hearts that the world in vain had tried,
And sorrow but more closely tied;
That stood the storm when waves were rough,
Yet in a sunny hour fall off,
Like ships that have gone down at sea
When heaven was all tranquillity.

THOMAS MOORE

January 8, 1845

Monsieur, the poor have not need of much to sustain them—they ask only for the crumbs that fall from the rich man's table. But if they are refused the crumbs they die of hunger. Nor do I, either, need much affection from those I love. I should not know what to do with a friendship entire and complete—I am not used to it. But you showed me of yore a little interest, when I was your pupil in Brussels, and I hold on to the maintenance of that little interest—I hold on to it as I would hold on to life.

While studying at the Pensionnat Heger in Brussels in 1842, **Charlotte Brontë** (1816–1855) fell deeply in love with its owner, Constantin Heger, but he was a married man and resolved never to respond to her schoolgirl crush. Later, she drew on her experiences with M. Heger in her third published novel, *Villette*.

He who loves 50 people has
50 woes; he who loves no
one has no woes.

BUDDHA

Between lovers a little confession
is a dangerous thing.

HELEN ROWLAND

You bid me write short to you and I have much to say. You also bade me believe that it was a fancy which made me cherish an attachment for you. It cannot be a fancy since you have been for the last year the object upon which every solitary moment led me to muse.

I do not expect you to love me, I am not worthy of your love. I feel you are superior, yet much to my surprise, more to my happiness, you betrayed passions I had believed no longer alive in your bosom. Shall I also have to ruefully experience the want of happiness? Shall I reject it when it is offered? I may appear to you imprudent, vicious; my opinions detestable, my theory depraved; but one thing, at least, time shall show you: that I love gently and with affection, that I am incapable of anything approaching to the feeling of revenge or malice; I do assure you, your future will shall be mine, and everything you shall do or say, I shall not question.

Another of **Lord Byron's** many women was Jane "Claire" Clairmont (1798–1879). In 1816, at the time that he was separating from his wife, Claire seduced him. The poet made it clear, however, that he did not want her, even when she announced that she was carrying his child. Byron took charge of the baby, named Allegra, and later, bored with fatherhood, entered her into a convent school, where she tragically died of typhus in 1822.

I broke my heart because of you, my dear;
I wept full many an unmanly tear—
But as in agony I lay awake
I thought, "What lovely poems this will make!"

HARRY KEMP

To say that you can love one person for your entire
life is like claiming that a candle will continue to
burn for as long as you live.

LEO TOLSTOY

Love ceases to be a pleasure,
when it ceases to be a secret.

APHRA BEHN

London, December 1842
or early 1843

Having loved you well enough to give you my life when it was best
work giving—having made you the center of all my hopes of
earthly happiness—having never loved any human being as I have
loved you, you can never be to me like any other human being, and it
is utterly impossible that I should ever regard you with indifference.

My whole existence having once had you for its sole object, and all
its thoughts, hopes, affections having, in their full harvest, been yours,
it is utterly impossible that I should ever forget this—that I should ever
forget that you were once my lover and are my husband and the father
of my children. I cannot behold you without emotion; my heart still
answers to your voice, my blood in my veins to your footsteps.

London-born actress and writer **Frances Anne "Fanny" Kemble** (1809–1893) met and married the American plantation owner Pierce Butler while on a tour of America in 1832, and left the theater to settle on his plantation in Georgia. It was a troubled and stormy relationship, as evidenced in this letter, which she wrote him in 1842 or 1843, and they divorced in 1848, after which she returned to her acting career.

The Peace of Wild Things

When despair grows in me
and I wake in the middle of the night at the least sound
in fear of what my life and my children's lives may be,
I go and lie down where the wood drake
rests in his beauty on the water, and the great heron feeds.
I come into the peace of wild things
who do not tax their lives with forethought
of grief. I come into the presence of still water.
And I feel above me the day-blind stars
waiting for their light. For a time
I rest in the grace of the world, and am free.

WENDELL BERRY

December 1847

I don't know anything dreadful enough to liken to you—you are like a sweet forest of pleasant glades and whispering branches—where people wander on and on in its playing shadows they know not how far—and when they come near the centre of it, it is all cold and impenetrable—and when they would fain turn, lo—they are hedged with briars and thorns and cannot escape . . .

You are like the bright—soft—swelling—lovely fields of a high glacier covered with fresh morning snow—which is heavenly to the eye—and soft and winning on the foot—but beneath, there are winding clefts and dark places in its cold—cold ice—where men fall, and rise not again.

This letter was written by the gifted if rather self-centered **John Ruskin** (1819–1900), British writer, critic, and reformer, to the demanding social climber Euphemia Chalmers Gray, usually known as "Effie," the year before they married. It is said that their marriage was never consummated. Whether or not this is true, the marriage certainly wasn't a success. Perhaps a glimpse of the reasons why is offered in the letter. . .

In a separation it is the one who is not really in love who says the more tender things.

MARCEL PROUST

Love, free as air at sight of human ties,
Spreads his light wings, and in a moment flies.

ALEXANDER POPE

Ashes of Life

Love has gone and left me and the days are all alike;
    Eat I must, and sleep I will,—and would that night were here!
But ah!—to lie awake and hear the slow hours strike!
    Would that it were day again!—with twilight near!

Love has gone and left me and I don't know what to do;
    This or that or what you will is all the same to me;
But all the things that I begin I leave before I'm through,—
    There's little use in anything as far as I can see.

Love has gone and left me,—and the neighbors knock and borrow,
    And life goes on forever like the gnawing of a mouse,—
And to-morrow and to-morrow and to-morrow and to-morrow
    There's this little street and this little house.

EDNA ST. VINCENT MILLAY.

lasting l♡ve

The most wonderful thing about love is that it can last forever. There are plenty of long-married couples who profess to adore each other as much as they did when they first met. The extracts in this section contain many examples of this kind of romantic success story, and show how true love can weather all storms and become even stronger.

Love, this is the great Faith!

ARTHUR RIMBAUD

And now these three remain: faith, hope and love.
But the greatest of these is love.

FROM *THE BIBLE*

Wondrous Moment

The wondrous moment of our meeting . . .
I well remember you appear
Before me like a vision fleeting,
A beauty's angel pure and clear.

In hopeless ennui surrounding
The worldly bustle, to my ear
For long your tender voice kept sounding,
For long in dreams came features dear.

Time passed. Unruly storms confounded
Old dreams, and I from year to year
Forgot how tender you had sounded,
Your heavenly features once so dear.

My backwoods days dragged slow and quiet—
Dull fence around, dark vault above—
Devoid of God and uninspired,
Devoid of tears, of fire, of love.

Sleep from my soul began retreating,
And here you once again appear
Before me like a vision fleeting,
A beauty's angel pure and clear.

In ecstasy the heart is beating,
Old joys for it anew revive;
Inspired and God-filled, it is greeting
The fire, and tears, and love alive.

ALEXANDER PUSHKIN

January 10, 1846

Do you know, when you have told me to think of you, I have been feeling ashamed of thinking of you so much, of thinking of only you—which is too much, perhaps. Shall I tell you? It seems to me, to myself, that no man was ever before to any woman what you are to me—the fulness must be in proportion, you know, to the vacancy . . . and only I know what was behind—the long wilderness without the blossoming rose . . . and the capacity for happiness, like a black gaping hole, before this silver flooding. Is it wonderful that I should stand as in a dream, and disbelieve—not you—but my own fate?

Was ever any one taken suddenly from a lampless dungeon and placed upon the pinnacle of a mountain, without the head turning round and the heart turning faint, as mine do? And you love me more, you say?—Shall I thank you or God? Both,—indeed—and there is no possible return from me to either of you! I thank you as the unworthy may, and as we all thank God. How shall I ever prove what my heart is to you? How will you ever see it as I feel it? I ask myself in vain. Have so much faith in me, my only beloved, as to use me simply for your own advantage and happiness, and to your own ends without a thought of any others—that is all I could ask you without any disquiet as to the granting of it—May God bless you!—Your B.A.

The romance between Robert Browning and **Elizabeth Barrett Browning** (1806–1861) began with a few words written by him in response to one of her poems and grew into an exchange of almost six hundred letters. Her father was bitterly opposed to their relationship so in 1846, the couple eloped to Florence, Italy. Her father never spoke to them again.

Young love is a flame; very pretty, often very
hot and fierce, but still only light and flickering.
The love of the older and disciplined heart is
as coals, deep-burning, unquenchable.

HENRY WARD BEECHER

My darling Clemmie,

In your letter from Madras you wrote some words very dear to me, about my having enriched your life. I cannot tell you what pleasure this gave me, because I always feel so overwhelmingly in your debt, if there can be accounts in love. . . . What it has been to me to live all these years in your heart and companionship no phrases can convey.

Time passes swiftly, but is it not joyous to see how great and growing is the treasure we have gathered together, amid the storms and stresses of so many eventful and to millions tragic and terrible years?

Your loving husband

From a brief stop in India, during a long sea voyage from England to Indonesia in January 1935, **Winston Churchill's** (1874–1965) wife Clementine wrote to her husband: "Oh my Darling, I'm thinking so much of you and how you have enriched my life. I have loved you very much but I wish I had been a more amusing wife to you. How nice it would be if we were young again." Winston's reply clearly reflects a love and devotion that lasted right up until the end.

She Comes Not

She comes not when Noon is on the roses—
Too bright is Day.
She comes not to the Soul till it reposes
From work and play.

But when Night is on the hills, and the great Voices
Roll in from Sea,
By starlight and candle-light and dreamlight
She comes to me.

HERBERT TRENCH

People often start by falling in love, and they go on for years without realizing that love must change into some other love which is so unlike it that it can hardly be recognized as love at all.

IRIS MURDOCH

The motto of chivalry is also the motto of wisdom; to serve all, but love only one.

HONORÉ DE BALZAC

When You Are Old

When you are old and grey and full of sleep,
And nodding by the fire, take down this book,
And slowly read, and dream of the soft look
Your eyes had once, and of their shadows deep;

How many loved your moments of glad grace,
And loved your beauty with love false or true,
But one man loved the pilgrim Soul in you,
And loved the sorrows of your changing face;

And bending down beside the glowing bars,
Murmur, a little sadly, how Love fled
And paced upon the mountains overhead
And hid his face amid a crowd of stars.

WILLIAM BUTLER YEATS

East Bergholt. February 27, 1816

I received your letter my ever dearest Maria, this morning. You know my anxious disposition too well not be aware how much I feel at this time. At the distance we are from each other every fear will obtrude itself on my mind. Let me hope that you are not really worse than your kindness, your affection, for me make you say. . . . I think . . . that no more molestation will arise to the recovery of your health, which I pray for beyond every other blessing under heaven.

Let us . . . think only of the blessings that providence may yet have in store for us and that we may yet possess. I am happy in love—an affection exceeding a thousand times my deserts, which has continued so many years, and is yet undiminished. . . . Never will I marry in this world if I marry not you. Truly can I say that for the seven years since I avowed my love for you, I have . . . foregone all company, and the society of all females (except my own relations) for your sake.

I am still ready to make my sacrifice for you. . . . I will submit to any thing you may command me—but cease to respect, to love and adore you I never can or will. I must still think that we should have married long ago—we should have had many troubles—but we have yet had no joys, and we could not have starved. . . . Your FRIENDS have never been without a hope of parting us and see what that has cost us both—but no more. Believe me, my beloved & ever dearest Maria, most faithfully yours, John

The English painter John Constable (1776–1837) was thirty-three when he met and fell in love with Maria Bicknell, whose family threatened her with disinheritance if she consented to marry him. They continued their clandestine courtship for seven years, until Constable's father died in 1816, leaving the painter with an income that made the couple's marriage possible.

Absence diminishes small loves and increases great ones, as the wind blows out the candle and blows up the bonfire.

FRANÇOIS, DUC DE LA ROCHEFOUCAULD

We are not the same persons this year as last; nor are those we love. It is a happy chance if we, changing, continue to love a changed person.

W. SOMERSET MAUGHAM

Y ou have been with me constantly, sweetheart. At Kangerdlooksoah I looked repeatedly at Ptarmigan Island and thought of the time we camped there. At Nuuatoksoah I landed where we were. And on the 11th we passed the mouth of Bowdoin Bay in brilliant weather, and as long as I could I kept my eyes on Anniversary Lodge. We have been great chums dear. Tell Marie to remember what I told her, tell "Mister Man" [Robert Peary Jr.] to remember "straight and strong and clean and honest," obey orders, and never forget that Daddy put "Mut" in his charge till he himself comes back to take her. In fancy I kiss your dear eyes and lips and cheeks sweetheart; and dream of you and my children, and my home till I come again. Kiss my babies for me. Aufwiedersehen.

Love, Love, Love. Your Bert

"I shall find a way or make one" is the motto on the grave that explorer **Robert Edwin Peary** (1856–1920) shares with his wife, Josephine Diebitsch. Peary made and survived many voyages to the Polar regions. Josephine was his greatest supporter, accompanying her husband on three of his expeditions.

Only until this cigarette is ended,
A little moment at the end of all,
While on the floor the quiet ashes fall,
And in the firelight to a lance extended,
Bizarrely with the jazzing music blended,
The broken shadow dances on the wall,
I will permit my memory to recall
The vision of you, by all my dreams attended.
And then adieu,—farewell!—the dream is done.
Yours is a face of which I can forget
The color and the features, every one,
The words not ever, and the smiles not yet;
But in your day this moment is the sun
Upon a hill, after the sun has set.

FROM *SECOND APRIL* > EDNA ST. VINCENT MILLAY

Women still remember the first kiss
after men have forgotten the last.

GOURMONT

I never knew how to worship until I knew how to love.

HENRY WARD BEECHER

The White House
September 19, 1915

My noble, incomparable Edith,

I do not know how to express or analyze the conflicting emotions that have surged like a storm through my heart all night long. I only know that first and foremost in all my thoughts has been the glorious confirmation you gave me last night—without effort, unconsciously, as of course—of all I have ever thought of your mind and heart.

You have the greatest soul, the noblest nature, the sweetest, most loving heart I have ever known, and my love, my reverence, my admiration for you, you have increased in one evening as I should have thought only a lifetime of intimate, loving association could have increased them.

You are more wonderful and lovely in my eyes than you ever were before; and my pride and joy and gratitude that you should love me with such a perfect love are beyond all expression, except in some great poem which I cannot write.

Your own,

Woodrow

Fate has a curious part to play in many romances, as it did for the widowed Edith Galt, who, through a string of mutual friendships, met the recently bereaved and still mourning U. S. president **Woodrow Wilson** (1856–1924). The lonely president took an instant liking to Mrs. Galt and they soon fell in love. The couple were married at her home on December 18, 1915.

Thus I wind myself
Into this willow garland, and am prouder
That I was once your love (though now
    refused)
Than to have had another true to me.

BEAUMONT AND FLETCHER (FRANCIS BEAUMONT AND JOHN FLETCHER)

It is love, not reason, that is stronger than death.

THOMAS MANN

For those who love, time is eternity.

HENRY VAN DYKE

But, my dear wife, when I know that with my own joys I lay down nearly all of yours, and replace them in this life with cares and sorrows—when, after having eaten for long years the bitter fruit of orphanage myself, I must offer it as their only sustenance to my dear little children—is it weak or dishonorable, while the banner of my purpose floats calmly and proudly in the breeze, that my unbounded love for you, my darling wife and children, should struggle in fierce, though useless, contest with my love of country?

I cannot describe to you my feelings on this calm summer night, when two thousand men are sleeping around me, many of them enjoying the last, perhaps, before that of death—and I, suspicious that Death is creeping behind me with his fatal dart, am communing with God, my country, and thee.

During the American Civil War, **Major Sullivan Ballou** (1829–1861) of the 2nd Rhode Island Volunteers wrote a letter home to his wife in Smithfield, Rhode Island, from which this passage is extracted. The letter is made all the more poignant by the fact that Sullivan, along with four thousand other soldiers, was to be killed a week later at the Battle of Bull Run.

December 31st, 1851

You have been wonderful, my Juliette, all through these dark and violent days. If I needed love, you brought it to me, bless you! When, in my hiding places, always dangerous, after a night of waiting, I heard the key of my door trembling in your fingers, peril and darkness were no longer round me—what entered then was light!

We must never forget those terrible, but so sweet, hours when you were close to me in the intervals of fighting. Let us remember all our lives that dark little room, the ancient hangings, the two armchairs, side by side, the meal we ate off the corner of the table, the cold chicken you had brought; our sweet converse, your caresses, your anxieties, your devotion. You were surprised to find me calm and serene. Do you know whence came both calmness and serenity? From you . . .

Victor Hugo first met the actress Juliette Drouet in 1833, the same year he became married to Adele Foucher. Juliette would remain his mistress for fifty years, and upon her death he stopped writing. He followed her to the grave two years later.

WHEN first, beloved, in vanished hours,
The Blind Man sought thy hand to gain,
They said thy cheek was bright as flowers
New freshened by the summer rain.
The beauty which made them rejoice,
My darkened eyes might never see;
But well I knew thy gentle voice,
And that was all in all to me.

At length, as years rolled swiftly on,
They talked to me of Time's decay,
Of roses from thy soft cheek gone,
Of ebon tresses turned to gray.
I heard them, but I heeded not
The withering change I could not see;
Thy voice still cheered my darkened lot,
And that was all in all to me.

And still, beloved, till life grows cold,
We'll wander 'neath the genial sky,
And only know that we grow old
By counting happy hours gone by.
Thy cheek may lose its blushing hue,
Thy brow less beautiful may be;
But, oh, the voice which first I knew
Still keeps the same sweet tone to me.

CAROLINE NORTON, LADY MAXWELL

index

A

Allen, Elizabeth Akers
86–7
Arnold, Matthew 10–1
Atwood, Margaret 153
Augustine, Saint 90

B

Baillie, Jane 146–7
Baldwin, James 79
Ballou, Major Sullivan
244–5
Balzac, Honoré de 118,
119, 225
Beaumont, Francis (with
John Fletcher) 240
Beecher, Henry Ward
218, 237
Behn, Aphra 176, 199
Bergman, Ingrid 85
Berry, Wendell 202
Bhagavad Gita 65
Bible, the 213
Bonaparte, Napoleon
138–9
Braque, Georges 68

Brontë, Charlotte 190–1
Brooke, Rupert 94–5
Browning, Elizabeth
Barrett 92, 216–7
Browning, Robert 168–9
Buddha 192
Byron, George Gordon,
Lord 106–7, 194–5

C

Carlyle, Thomas 85
Chevalier, Maurice 27
Churchill, Randolph S.
70–1, 220–1
Cofer, Judith Ortiz 158
Coleridge, Samuel Taylor
103
Colton, Charles Caleb
178
Constable, John 228–9
Creeley, Robert 12, 36,
140
Curie, Pierre 58–9

D

Dickinson, Emily 100

Duras, Marguerite 126

E

Einstein, Albert 9
Emerson, Ralph Waldo
127

F

Flaubert, Gustave 62–3,
155
Fletcher, John (with
Francis Beaumont) 240
Franklin, Benjamin 16
French proverb 69
Freud, Sigmund 51

G

Gandhi, Mahatma 46
Gay, John 173
Gibler, Colley 91
Gide, André 97
Goethe, Johann
Wolfgang von 66–7
Gourmont 236
Graves, Robert 148–9
Guitry, Sacha 165, 185

H

Haliburton, Thomas C. 41
Hawthorne, Nathaniel
52–3
Herrick, Robert 42–3,
105
Hugo, Victor 102, 112–3,
246–7

J

Jonson, Ben 76

K

Kafka, Franz 74–5
Keats, John 182–3
Kemble, Frances Anne
"Fanny" 200–1
Kemp, Harry 196
Khayyam, Omar 72

L

La Rochefoucauld,
François, duc de 13, 230
Lao-Tzu 110
Liszt, Franz 28–9
Ludwig, Emil 46

M

McCarthy, Mary 54–5
McLaughlin, Mignon
130
Mann, Thomas 242
Mansfield, Katharine
98–9
Maugham, W. Somerset
231
Maxwell, Caroline
Norton, Lady 248–9
Meredith, George 184
Millay, Edna St. Vincent
208, 234
Milton, John 166
Mirabeau, Comte de
172–3
Moore, Pamela 44–5
Moore, Thomas 188
Mozart, Wolfgang
Amadeus 142–3
Murdoch, Iris 224
Musset, Alfred de 14–5

N

Neruda, Pablo 115

Nietzsche, Friedrich 110

O

Otway, Thomas 186–7
Ovid 96, 131, 156–7

P

Pascal, Blaise 30, 50
Pavese, Cesare 145
Peary, Robert Edwin
232–3
Poe, Edgar Allan 24–5
Pope, Alexander 207
Proust, Marcel 206
Pushkin, Alexander 181,
214–5

R

Raleigh, Sir Walter
132–3
Rexroth, Kenneth 33
Rimbaud, Arthur 212
Robison, Philip 26
Roethke, Theodore 179
Rowland, Helen 8, 193
Ruskin, John 204–5

Russell, Bertrand 22, 61

S

Sandburg, Carl 34–5, 160
Sarton, May 154
Sayre, Zelda 134–5
Schumann, Robert 38–9
Sexton, Anne 108–9
Shakespeare, William 16
Shaw, George Bernard
  120–1
Shelley, Percy Bysshe
  80–1
Stendhal 23

Sterne, Laurence 122–3
Stowe, Harriet Beecher
  162-3

T

Tennyson, Alfred, Lord
  19, 136-7, 150
Thackeray, William
  Makepeace 172
Tolstoy, Leo 41, 124, 198
Trench, Herbert 222

V

Van Dyke, Henry 243

Voltaire 56

W

Wilde, Oscar 60, 144, 164
Wilson, Woodrow 238–9
Wordsworth, Mary 82–3

Y

Yeats, W. B. 20–1, 117,
  227
Yourcenar, Marguerite
  78

acknowledgments

pp. 20–21 "The Young Man's Song," p. 117 **"A Drinking Song,"** p. 227 **"When You Are Old"** by W. B. Yeats, from RESPONSIBILITIES AND OTHER POEMS (Macmillan, 1916). Used by permission of A. P. Watt on behalf of Michael B. Yeats. Reprinted with the permission of Scribner, an imprint of Simon & Schuster Adult Publishing Group, from THE COLLECTED WORKS OF W. B. YEATS, VOLUME 1: THE POEMS, REVISED, edited by Richard J. Finneran. (New York: Scribner, 1997).

p. 33 "The Love Poems of Marichiko: IV" by Kenneth Rexroth, from THE MORNING STAR, copyright © 1979 by Kenneth Rexroth. Reprinted by permission of New Directions Publishing Corp.

pp. 34–35 "Under the Harvest Moon" from CHICAGO POEMS by Carl Sandburg, copyright 1916 by Holt, Rinehart and Winston and renewed 1944 by Carl Sandburg, reprinted by permission of Harcourt, Inc.

p. 36 "Here," p. 140 **"Ballad of the Despairing Husband"** by Robert Creeley, from COLLECTED POEMS OF ROBERT CREELEY, 1945–1975. Copyright © 1983 The Regents of the University of California. Reprinted by permission of University of California Press and Marion Boyars Publishers Ltd.

pp. 44–45 Reprinted by the kind permission of Mrs Pamela Ruffoni and the Trustess of the Imperial War Museum.

pp. 54–55 By permission of the Mary McCarthy Literary Trust.

pp. 108–109 "When Man Enters Woman," from THE AWFUL ROWING TOWARD GOD by Anne Sexton. Copyright © 1975 by Loring Conant, Jr., Executor of the Estate of Anne Sexton. Reprinted by permission of Houghton Mifflin Company. All rights reserved.

p. 115 "Naked," from FIVE DECADES: Poems 1925–1970 by Pablo Neruda, translated by Ben Belitt. Copyright © by Ben Belitt. Used by permission of Grove/Atlantic, Inc.

PICTURE CREDITS

p. 31 *Woman in Love,* 1856 by Henry Nelson O'Neil (1817-80) Phillips, The International Fine Art Auctioneers, UK/Bridgeman Art Library

p. 40 *Ask me no more,* 1906 (oil on canvas) by Sir Lawrence Alma-Tadema (1836-1912) Private Collection/Bridgeman Art Library

p. 47 *Lovers on a Balcony* by Georges Barbier © Stapleton Collection/CORBIS

p. 57 *Promenade,* 1913 (oil on canvas) by Marc Chagall (1887-1985) State Russian Museum, St. Petersburg, Russia/Bridgeman Art Library © ADAGP, Paris and DACS, London 2002

p. 73 *Pair of Lovers* by Pal Szinyei-Merse © Archivo Iconografico, S.A./CORBIS

p. 84 *The Kiss* by Francesco Hayez (1791-1882) The Art Archive/Galleria Brera Milan/Dagli Orti (A)

p. 101 *The Fisherman and the Syren:* From a Ballad by Goethe, c.1856-58 by Frederic Leighton (1830-96) Bristol City Museum and Art Gallery, UK/Bridgeman Art Library

p. 116 *The Kiss* by Theodore Jacques Ralli © Christie's Images/CORBIS

p. 125 *Daphnis and Chloë,* 1913 by Gabriel Deluc The Art Archive/Musée Maurice Ravel Montfort-L'Amaury/Dagli Orti

p. 141 *The Bride,* 1886 *(w/c on paper)* by Anders Leonard Zorn (1860-1920) National museum, Stockholm, Sweden/Bridgeman Art Library

p. 152 *The engaged couple, or The Sisley Family,* 1868 *(oil on canvas)* by Pierre Auguste Renoir (1841-1919) Wallraf-Richartz Museum, Cologne, Germany/Bridgeman Art Library

p. 167 *The Proposal,* 1853 *(oil on panel)* by William Powell Frith (1819-1909) Private Collection/Bridgeman Art Library

p. 180 *Boer War, 1900 - 'Last Summer Things Were Greener,'* 1901 (oil on canvas) by John Byam Liston Shaw (1872-1919) Birmingham Museums and Art Gallery/Bridgeman Art Library

p. 189 *Disappointed love,* 1821 by Francis Danby (1793-1861) Victoria & Albert Museum, London, UK/Bridgeman Art Library

p. 197 *Les Adieux,* 1871 *(oil on canvas)* by James Jacques Joseph Tissot (1836-1902) Bristol City Museum and Art Gallery, UK/Bridgeman Art Library

p. 223 *A Couple on Horseback Beside a Moonlit Lake* *(tempera on panel)* by Mark Briscoe (Contemporary Artist) Private Collection/Bridgeman Art Library

p. 241 *Dance at Bougival,* 1882-3 by Pierre Auguste Renoir (1841-1919) Museum of Fine Arts, Boston, Massachusetts, MA, USA/Bridgeman Art Library